STAN MACK'S REAL LIFE FUNNIES

Guarantee: All Dialogue Is Reported Verbatim

STAN MACK'S REAL LIFE FUNNIES

Guarantee: All Dialogue Is Reported Verbatim

by Stan Mack

G. P. Putnam's Sons
New York, N.Y.

Copyright ©1979 by Stan Mack

All rights reserved. This book or parts thereof must not be reproduced in
any form without permission.
All cartoons herein originally appeared in *The Village Voice*.

SBN: (cloth edition) 399-12273-7

SBN: (paper edition) 399-12306-7

Library of Congress Cataloging in Publication Data

Mack, Stanley.
   Stan Mack's Real life funnies.

   "All comic strips herein originally appeared in the Village Voice."
   I. Title.   II. Title: Real life funnies.
PN6728.R4M3   741.5'973   78-22071

PRINTED IN THE UNITED STATES OF AMERICA

Introduction

Talk about midlife crisis . . . I walked into one at the age of 37. I was a comic illustrator and editorial art director with a secret ambition to get unglued from my drawing board and go out into the world to draw. But as an art director, I knew comic illustrators rarely received reportage assignments. Photographers covered conventions, demonstrations, political events, awards presentations and bars.

One day I talked a *New York Times* editor into letting me accompany a reporter on a feature story assignment. The story was a light piece about some garden club women touring various corporate headquarters and peering into executive boardrooms and washrooms. I jotted down some comments I overheard while I was sketching. The reporter, Georgia Dullea, thought they were funny, so we included the comments in the cartoons that accompanied her story. A *writer* liked *my* quotes!

That was the beginning of my strange new career. Why not, I thought, wander into all sorts of places and events, write down what people said, and sketch the people and surroundings while I listened? I discussed the idea with Milton Glazer at the *Village Voice*. He liked the idea and suggested that a strip run regularly in the *Voice*. I suspect that he made the suggestion more in a spirit of adventure than of confidence.

On my first assignment for the *Voice*, I hung around Bloomingdale's for a few nights, scribbling and sketching. I didn't feel at all like a journalist that night. I had a nervous stomach and felt like a snoop. And when the sales people began giving me suspicious looks it was time to move on. I went home and put it together into a sort of comic strip. I've always enjoyed telling comic stories in sequence so it was natural for me to use this form.

I began going to places where I obviously did not belong and listening to people about whom I've always been curious: miracle healers, theater people, bums, politicians . . . men, women . . .

I began to develop a system. Carry a little pad and pencil. Dress to blend in quietly. Get to the destination in enough time to case the joint. It helps to be not too tall, not too short, not too dark, not too light, not too handsome, not too ugly, not too old and not too young. All of these I am, and it finally paid off, although I'm getting grey and wrinkled and can no longer fit in with the under 30 singles crowd. When I arrive, if I find that everybody

continued

knows each other, I make a quick exit and forget it. Otherwise, the system continues: smile and keep your ears open. Find the men's room (always good for a line), find coffee and food, which is very helpful unless you are trying to take notes. Look for a few convenient corners in which to hide. Learn to walk backwards in order to get closer to groups. Learn to stand in the middle of a mob and like it. And, finally, learn to change direction suddenly in order to follow a good line floating by. All of this, by the way, may make you horribly conspicuous rather than the invisible man, but what the hell. Appear preoccupied. If you are engaged in conversation, pay no attention to what you are saying. Say anything. Fake it. You can't listen and think at the same time. Float through the event. Each has its own particular current. Professional wrestlers and East Side gallery-hoppers move at different speeds. Hang around until it's over or until your feet hurt. Or until you just can't stand it another second. Wait for the last great line, settle for something less, and leave. Do not rush home. Put your notes away safely and go somewhere to decompress. I have had to rush home and produce a strip without sleep because of the deadline. Once it was after a St. Patrick's Day parade and evening—a long night not to be repeated except perhaps in wartime.

Problems do occur when you hang out where you don't belong. None has been violent so far—although once while I was sketching at a hotrod show, a big, beefy guy came towards me. I was sure he was on his way over to do violence. I considered eating my pad as he came closer. But he only wanted to sell me one of his "authentic, original, bullet-riddled Godfather cars before I copied his and built my own. I was asked to leave at the Pottery Barn, where they thought I was casing the joint. And at a fancy antiques show, a woman with a lot to hide or lose was positive that I was a CIA agent.

When I start to draw a strip, I sit with my deadline approaching and a pad full of quotes and doodles. I try to draw the kind of people who actually said the lines. It's amazing how much fashion, gesture and mental attitude change physical appearance. Take the same basic build—if that person who owns it dresses and thinks like the upper East Side gallery-goer, he or she will appear to be built quite differently from the upper West Side chess player.

I don't know why some comments seem important and others dull, but I know that it isn't until I begin to edit the material, laying the scraps of paper end to end, and draw the people that the story emerges. It's often a surprise. At a serious conference of intellectuals (a funny idea), for example, the comments of the participants became the background for a lament by a young woman about the problems of having intellectual boyfriends. At a sail-gliding exhibition, the glider pilot, who was supposed to do tricks in the air, picked up a strong tailwind, flew over the right shoulder of the Statue of Liberty, and disappeared. The comic strip turned out to be the story of an event that never happened. It's the unexpected that makes it work. Therefore it helps to approach everything with an open mind and no preconceptions, whether it involves policemen or transsexuals or frisbee addicts. This book is filled with ideas that first surprised me and later made sense.

And now if you'll excuse me, I have an event to cover. . . .

STAN MACK'S REAL LIFE FUNNIES

Guarantee: All Dialogue Is Reported Verbatim

Teatime

"I picked up this old lady a few weeks ago at the Opera House and took her to the East 70s. I mean she was really old — about 80 — but dressed beautifully."

"Anyway, we're riding along and she lights up a joint. Well, you know, everybody lights up joints in my cab, and I don't think anything of it."

"But this was an 80-year-old chick. So I turned to her and said, 'Excuse me, but is that some fancy European cigarette?'"

"She looked at me and said, 'Shmuck! Can't you tell good grass when you smell it?'"

"Can you believe it? I went home and told my wife that we should get some for her old man."

"I asked her where she got the grass and she said, 'From my niece. Every time she comes home from college she brings me a bag.'"

An Evening with a Male Liberationist

"Oh! Calcutta!" Casting Call

Extraterrestrials

Snow Job

Bug Watch in Rye, New York

Singles' Rap Session

Nursing Home New Year's Eve Party

Bloomingdale's

Road Company Rehearsal of "Let My People Come"

An Art Sale In Suburbia

It's a Dog's Life

Brian Auger at the Bottom Line

A Rolfer Lectures

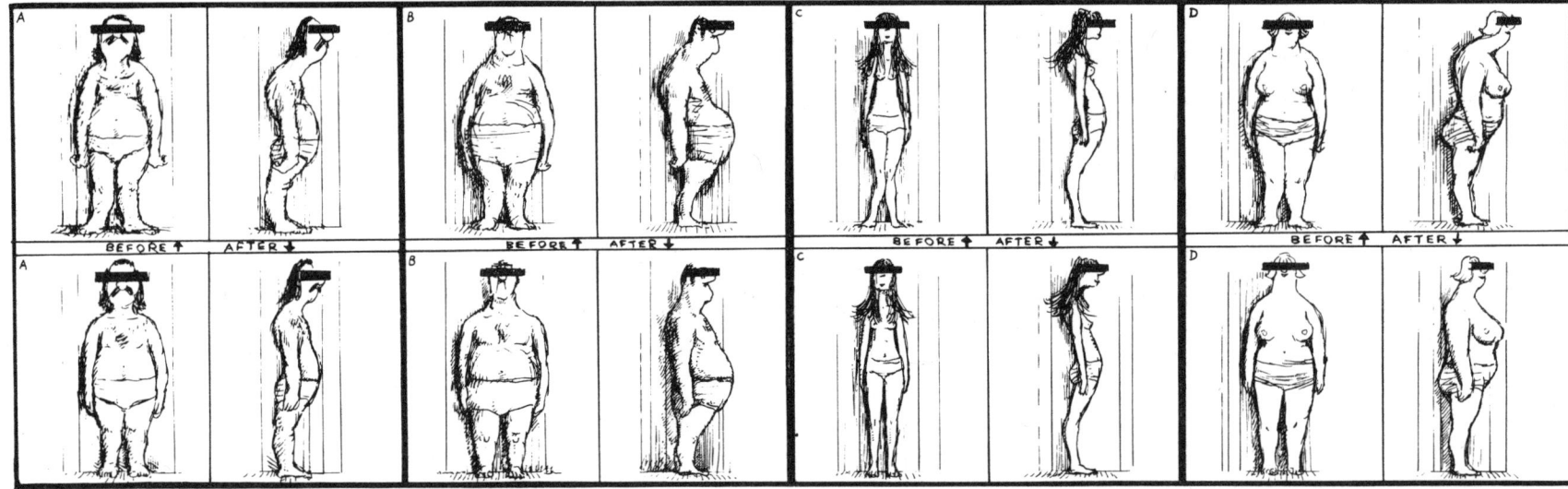

Rolfing tries to re-organize the body to keep itself up. It gets the blocks one on top of the other. A body that looks disorganized on the outside won't be ordered on the inside...

...If you look at people their necks stick forward... they weren't born that way, they're **DEFORMED!** In our sessions we start on the surface and go deeper an' deeper— like peeling an onion...

...Our culture is a head culture. The body only carries the head around. Some of us are born more upright than others. Rolfing gets the monkey out of man...

...Here is a slide of a Greek sculpture showing bad posture. Here is a slide of an Egyptian statue. This statue has it together! A beautiful Rolfed Egyptian body!...

...Rolfing isn't painful in the sense of pain!! The Eskimos have 50 words for snow. We have ONE! It's the same with pain. Can you describe what SEX is like?

...It's very individual. I may have to pull tissue **IN** with one person, pull it **OUT** with another. You don't **BUST** into muscles, you delicately, sensitively, manipulate them...

Rolfing takes away the junk you've suffered with for 30-40 years. Some people give off such bad toxins we have to burn epsom salts to clear the air...
© stan mack 2/77

...If a body is used to being distorted, can it resume a vertical position? A crude analogy is the body is like wet cement after Rolfing...

The bigger the person, the longer the session. Before a session I have an intention of what I expect. But sometimes I'm surprised. The body goes somewhere else...

Once you get into medical school you have to be an **IDIOT** not to graduate. Rolfing's not like that. It's younger and we only put out competent people. Our standards are high!

Press Conference: Bayh Bows Out

Two City Stories

Panel 1: WHAT A MISER.

Panel 2: LIVES IN A DUMP. TWO ROOMS FOR FIFTEEN DOLLARS.

Panel 3: NEVER EATS ANYTHING BUT BREAD, JAM, AND PEAS. BOUGHT HIS WIFE A DRESS FOR A DOLLAR.

Panel 4: SLEEPS EVERY AFTERNOON FROM THREE TO EIGHT. LIVES ON TWO CUPS OF COFFEE A DAY.

Panel 5: HE WON'T LEND YOU A DOLLAR.

Panel 6: I DON'T KNOW WHETHER TO LIE DOWN.

Panel 7: I MIGHT NOT GET UP.

Panel 8: I DON'T KNOW WHETHER I'M TIRED...

Panel 9: ... OR WHAT.

mack 8/75

Class Critique at Parsons

A Stroll Through the Magic Kingdom

Macy's Toyland

Inside CBS:
The Maryland/Michigan Primaries

Bob McAllister's Children's Show at Grossinger's—Jan. 24th

Indoor Activities at Grossinger's

1. Right to Lifers View Sex Education Movie
2. Opening of an Erotic-Art Show

N.Y. State Democrats Meet with Carter at the Statler Hilton—June 14

Larcada Gallery Graphics Exhibit

New Yorkers Welcome the Convention, July 1976

1 "THE CITY IS STROKIN' THE PUBLIC."

"THERE'S GONNA BE TROUBLE DURING THE CONVENTION."

"THE ONLY THING THAT WILL KEEP US FROM HAVING TROUBLE IS **TORRENTIAL RAINS!**"

"THE ONLY THING THE CITY DOESN'T WANT IS A RIOT IN HARLEM."

"WELL, GOTTA GO GET THIS GUY'S STOMACH PUMPED OUT."

2 "WE SHOULD DO BUSINESS. THEY'RE HUMAN LIKE EVERYONE ELSE."

"I USE'TA WORK FOR PLANNED PARENTHOOD, HANDING OUT PAPER."

"'TILL THE MASSAGE PARLOR OFFERED ME A BETTER DEAL."

"I WORK TWELVE HOURS A DAY. I'M WAITIN' FOR SOME COMMUTER TO OFFER ME A JOB 'CAUSE THEY SEE I'M RELIABLE."

"I GOTTA MOVE. HERE COMES AN OFFICER. THEY'RE BUSTIN' MY CHOPS."

© Stan Mack 7/76

1. Final Hours of Democratic Convention
2. Post-Convention Scene, Penn Station

Symposium on Marriage at St. John the Divine

Waiting for Seats at the Hearst Trial

A Seat at the Hearst Trial

Views from and of the Suburbs

Animal Lovers Picket "Missouri Breaks"

Cuckoos and a Clock

My roommate's hard of hearing. He wears a hearing aid without a battery. It's like talking to the wall.

He's got an Irish brogue and he's toothless. I can't understand a word he's saying.

Once in a while I nod or shake my head.

There's so many cuckoos running around loose.

Here's the way I see it. Ya see that clock up there? Man put it together so it'll go around and tell us the time.

It's like the universe. The moon goes around the earth, and the earth goes around the sun.

Well, I figure, if someone put that clock together, then someone must have put the universe together...

...right?

Walking Tour: SoHo Art through Anarchist Eyes

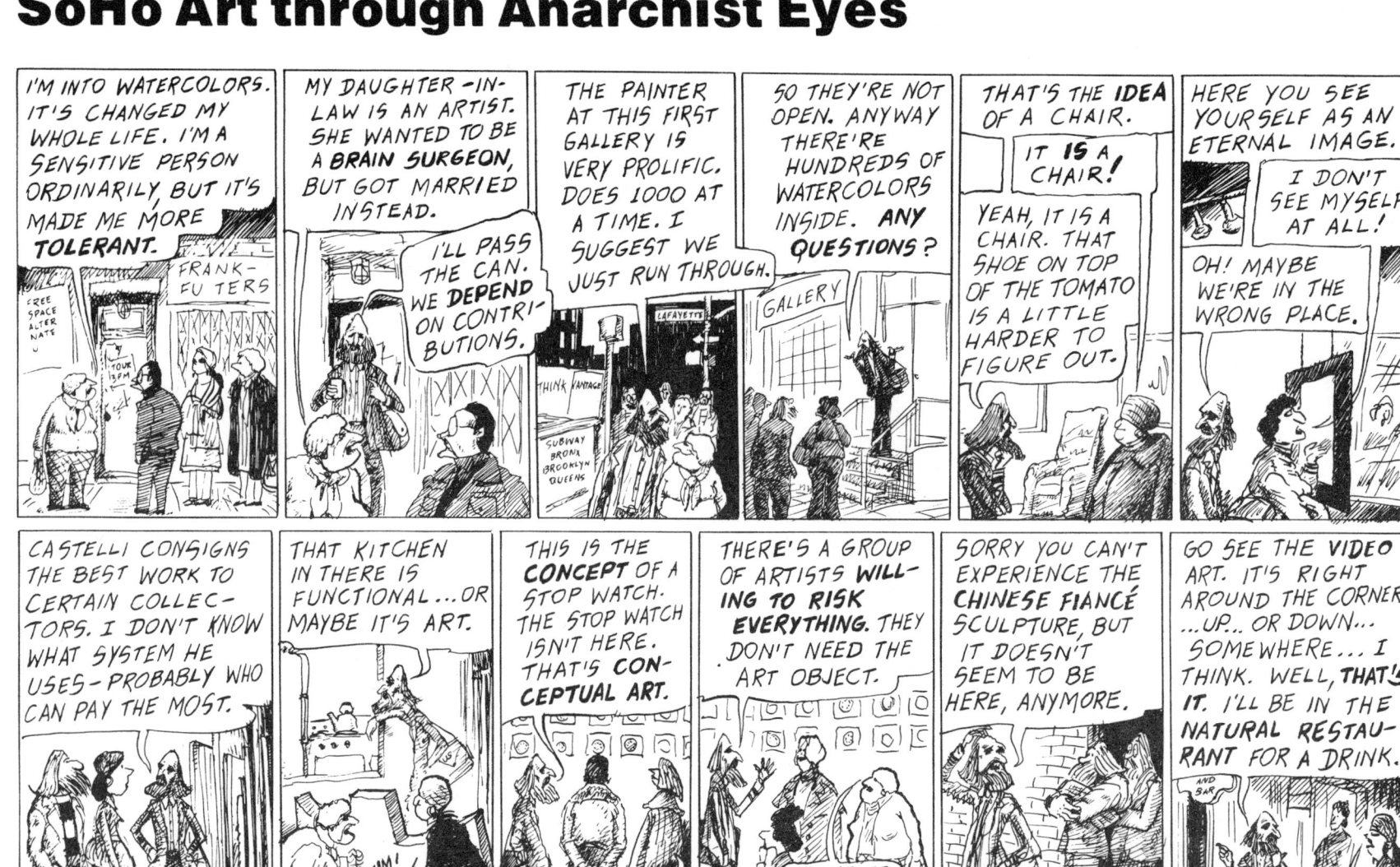

Thanksgiving Weekend, Port Authority

Report from a Friend: Grand Central Station Ladies Lounge

An Almost Perfect Life. . .

Moonpeople's Bicentennial Festival at Yankee Stadium—June 1

1. Suburban Scene
2. Urban Scene

City Voices

Lodge Fundraiser & Stag Show—Nov. 7

Three Vignettes

At NOW Headquarters and Egyptian Gardens

Verbal Noncommunication

Vernal Equinox at the Hayden Planetarium

Between the Acts

Kicking Off Ms. All-Bare Week

The Modern Language Association Conference at the Hilton

"All About Divorce" at Madison Square Garden

Adventure of a Commuter

Family Circles

Lessons in Product Development

Winter Antiques Show at the Armory

Westminster Dog Show at the Garden

The Lehman Wing

Cuny Opens, Fall 1976: Advanced Graffiti, 101

WHEN GOD CREATED MAN, ALL THE PARTS OF THE BODY ARGUED OVER WHO WAS GOING TO BE THE BOSS. THE BRAIN EXPLAINED THAT SINCE HE CONTROLLED ALL THE PARTS OF THE BODY HE SHOULD BE BOSS. THE EARS SAID THAT SINCE THEY ALLOWED MAN TO

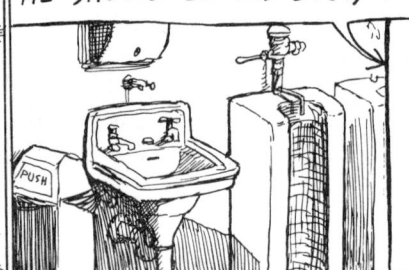

SEE THEY SHOULD BE BOSS. THE LEGS SAID SINCE THEY TOOK THE BODY WHEREVER IT WANTED TO GO THEY SHOULD BE THE BOSS. THE HANDS SAID NO, SINCE THEY DID ALL THE WORK THEY SHOULD BE BOSS. WHEN THE ASSHOLE SAID HE SHOULD BE THE BOSS, ALL

THE OTHER PARTS OF THE BODY LAUGHED. THIS MADE THE ASSHOLE IRATE AND CLOG ITSELF. THIS LASTED FOR ABOUT 3 DAYS. DURING THIS TIME THE BRAIN BECAME FOGGED, THE EYES BECAME CROSSED, THE LEGS BECAME WEAK AND COULD NO LONGER HOLD

UP THE BODY AND THE HANDS LAID LIMP AT THE SIDE OF THE BODY. IN ORDER TO GET RELIEF ALL THE PARTS OF THE BODY GAVE IN AND LET THE ASSHOLE BE THE BOSS. THIS SHOWS THAT YOU DON'T HAVE TO BE A BRAIN TO BE BOSS. YOU JUST HAVE TO BE AN ASSHOLE.

HI, MY NAME IS RITA, I WORK ON A FARM, I MAKE 3 PESOS A DAY, I GO TO SIN WITH RICHY HE GIVE ME SOME DICK HE TAKE ALL MY PESOS

I HAVE A PROBLEM I LOVE MY HUSBAND VERY MUCH BUT I ALSO LOVE HIS SISTER WHAT SHOULD I DO?

FOR A GOOD BLOW JOB CALL --- ---- ASK FOR SUSAN AND ASK FOR STUDENT RATES.

FOR A GREAT BLOW JOB CALL GORILLA --- ---- ANYTIME.

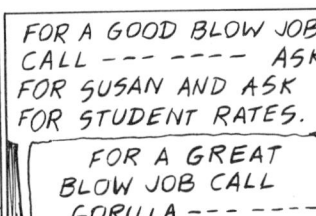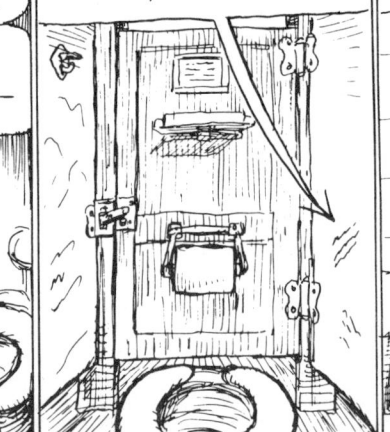

TO DO IS TO BE DESCARTE TO BE IS TO DO SARTRE DO BE DO, BE DO SINATRA

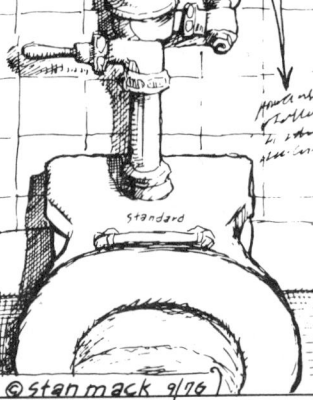

YOU ARE SITTING IN THE POETS' HALL OF FAME.

© stan mack 9/76

Senior Citizens at Large

Walk of the Town

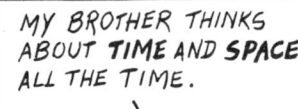

Women's Language

Short Takes

Fear of Landing

New York City Intellectuals Meet

Occult Festival

Creative Writing

I HAVE A FRIEND WHO HAS ALWAYS WANTED TO WRITE.

SHE GOT WORK AS AN EDITOR AT "VIVA", BUT SHE DIDN'T LIKE IT BECAUSE SHE'S NOT AN UPTOWN PERSON.

THEN THIS PERSON AT THE SOHO NEWS OFFERED HER A JOB AT A RIDICULOUSLY LOW SALARY.

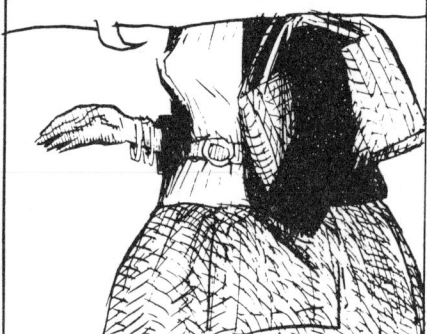
SHE SAID SHE'D TAKE THE RIDICULOUSLY LOW SALARY IF SHE COULD HAVE EDITORIAL FREEDOM.

SHE WANTED TO WRITE A MISS LONELYHEARTS COLUMN. SO I WROTE THE LETTERS AND SHE ANSWERED THEM.

SOMETIMES I MAKE THEM UP AND SOMETIMES I TELL ABOUT SOMEONE ELSE'S TROUBLES.

OH, SHE'LL RUN REAL ONES IF THEY'RE PRINTABLE AND INTERESTING. IT JUST MAKES IT MORE...

... REAL, Y'KNOW? SHE WRITES TERRIFIC BITCHY ANSWERS.

©stan mack 1/10/77

A Night with the "Single Again"

Short Takes

An Evening with R. Crumb and His Cheap Suit Serenaders at the School of Visual Arts

The World Body Building Show at Hunter College

Eros 75

Bob & Rick & Ted & Larry

Wrestling at the White Plains Country Center

Nancy's Letters from Camp

Buckley Headquarters—Aug. 11

The 1976 Republican Convention in Kansas City

continued

continued

continued

Cocktail Hour at Charlie Brown's

Sex Talk

Saturday in SoHo

Elevator Antics

Gallery Opening

Building a Downhill Racer, Part I

Building a Downhill Racer, Part II

Did You Know That . . . ?

Comic Book Convention at the Statler Hilton

Close Encounters at a Christmas Party

Two Sex Scenes: Westchester and Manhattan

Speaking of Medicaid . . .

Friday Night at Maxwell's Plum

Rally Against Crime

At the Super Market

St. Patrick's Day

Creativity in Advertising

An Introductory Session for SmokEnders

Minority Language

A Publisher Tests Its War Games

Benefit for Outward Bound at the Plaza

New England Beach Scene

New Year's Day at WBAI

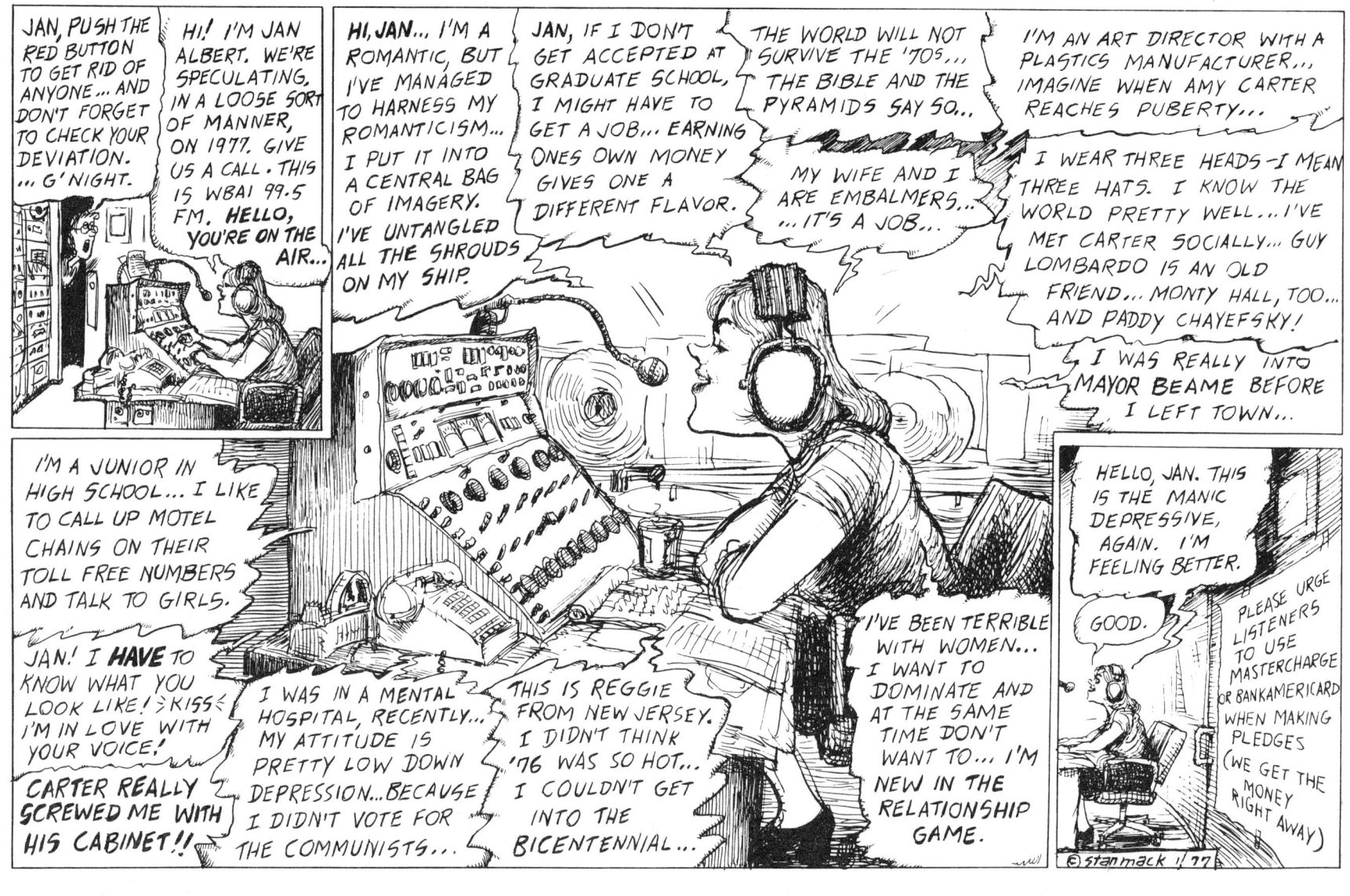

October Bargains on Fifth Avenue

Oh Men, Oh Women

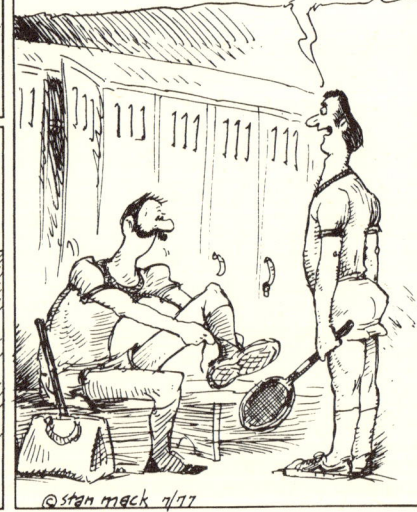

Cabinet à la Turque

Big Shots

Overbites

A La Recherche du Cabinet à la Turque (II)

It was right after the war... in Paris. The cabinet à la turque was on the first floor of our building. There was a real bathroom on the third floor.

A Russian immigrant lived next door to it. His name was Edward. He wore knickers and acted as if he were part of the aristocracy.

He got very angry because he claimed someone always was plugging up the toilet and nobody would admit it.

So he took the bathroom door off. If you wanted to use the bathroom, you had to ask Edward for the door. That way he thought he'd find out who plugged up the toilet.

You had to go in and say, "Edward, can I have the door?"

Between the cabinet à la turque and Edward, I was more constipated in that place...

Divorced Men Explore the Male Mystique

Towering Inferno

Cable Comes to SoHo

Pas de Trois

Walk of the Town

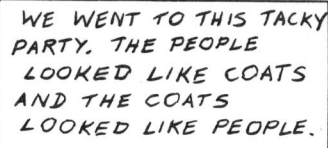

Party Patter

X-Rated

Matter Over Mind

Person to Person

Invitational Cat Show at the Garden—Mar. 20-21

Heavy Doings

A Professional Cartoonist Speaks to Art Students

Comediennes Backstage

Life Drawing

Selling Darth Vader

Singles' Rap Session at the Universalist Church

A Nonpartisan Business

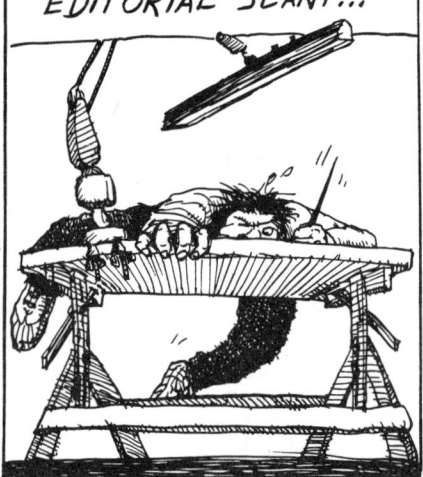

A Day at a Pigeon Show

The Divorce

Teed Off

An American Tragedy

Yale's Marching Band at Harvard-Yale Game

Paul Takes Over

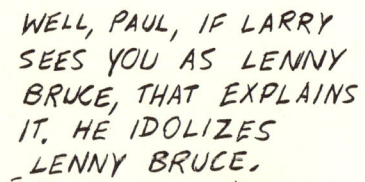

Suburban Toy Store After Christmas

Leroy Jenkins Crusade NYC: September 26

One for the Road: A Bar in Kissimmee, Florida

THE LAST TIME I SAW NEW YORK, I WAS IN THE NAVY. IT WAS RIGHT AFTER WORLD WAR II. I WAS SEVENTEEN.

MY BUDDY AND I WERE SITTING ON A BENCH IN CENTRAL PARK. THERE WAS THIS WEIRDO-LOOKING GUY ON THE NEXT BENCH HOLDING A SACK OF ORANGES.

HE CAME OVER TO US AND SAID, EXCUSE ME, WOULD YOU DO ME A FAVOR?

HE WAS A FAIRY! I KNEW WHAT HE WANTED. I WAS SUPPOSED TO BE A TOUGH SAILOR. I SAID SHOVE OFF!

HE SAID NO, NO! IT'S NOT WHAT YOU THINK. I'LL GIVE YOU TEN DOLLARS APIECE IF YOU THROW THESE ORANGES AT ME.

AT FIRST WE SAID NO. BUT AFTER AWHILE MY BUDDY SAID, Y'KNOW, WE COULD USE THAT TWENTY BUCKS. SO WE WENT OVER AND TOLD HIM WE'D DO IT.

WE THREW ALL THE ORANGES AT THE GUY. IT WAS HARD TO THROW — WE WERE FALLING DOWN LAUGHING. THE GUY KEPT YELLING, HARDER! FASTER! WE HIT HIM PRETTY GOOD.

I AGREE WITH THAT GUY WHO SAID NEW YORK IS A NICE PLACE TO VISIT, BUT I WOULDN'T WANT TO LIVE THERE.

© stan mack 3/77

The Voice Goes to Bed with a New Face

Parenting in the Suburbs

Lunch in Greenwich Village

Chain Letter

 "TRUST IN THE LORD WITH ALL YOUR HEART AND WILL, AND ACKNOWLEDGE, AND HE WILL LIGHT THE WAY." THIS PRAYER HAS BEEN SENT TO YOU FOR GOOD LUCK...

 ... YOU ARE TO RECEIVE GOOD LUCK WITHIN FOUR DAYS OF RECEIVING THIS LETTER. THIS IS NO JOKE... THIS CHAIN WAS WRITTEN BY A MISSIONARY FROM SO. AMERICA...

 ... YOU MUST HAVE 20 COPIES, IDENTICAL TO THIS ONE, AND SEND TO PEOPLE YOU THINK NEED GOOD LUCK. DO NOT KEEP THIS LETTER. IT MUST LEAVE YOU WITHIN 96 HOURS... AND SEE WHAT HAPPENS TO YOU ON THE FOURTH DAY... YOU WILL GET A SURPRISE...

 TAKE NOTE OF THE FOLLOWING: AN RAF OFFICER RECEIVED $10,000. DON ELLIOT RECEIVED $50,000, BUT LOST IT BECAUSE HE BROKE THE CHAIN... GEN. WALSH LOST HIS LIFE SIX DAYS AFTER HE RECEIVED THIS LETTER. HE FAILED TO CIRCULATE THIS PRAYER. HOWEVER, BEFORE HIS DEATH, HE RECEIVED $775,000...

 CONSTATION DIAZ ASKED HIS SECRETARY TO SEND 20 COPIES, AND HE WON A LOTTERY FOR 2 MILLION... CARLO CRODIET, AN OFFICE EMPLOYEE, FORGOT THE CHAIN AND LOST HIS JOB. HE FOUND THE CHAIN AND SENT IT TO 20 PEOPLE. FIVE DAYS AFTER HE GOT AN EVEN BETTER JOB.

 DOVER MORCHIA RECEIVED THE CHAIN, AND NOT BELEIVING IN IT, THREW IT AWAY. NINE DAYS LATER, HE DIED. FOR NO REASON WHAT SO EVER SHOULD THIS CHAIN BE BROKEN.

Her First Tennis Lesson

Sex Accessories

Blooming Asparagus

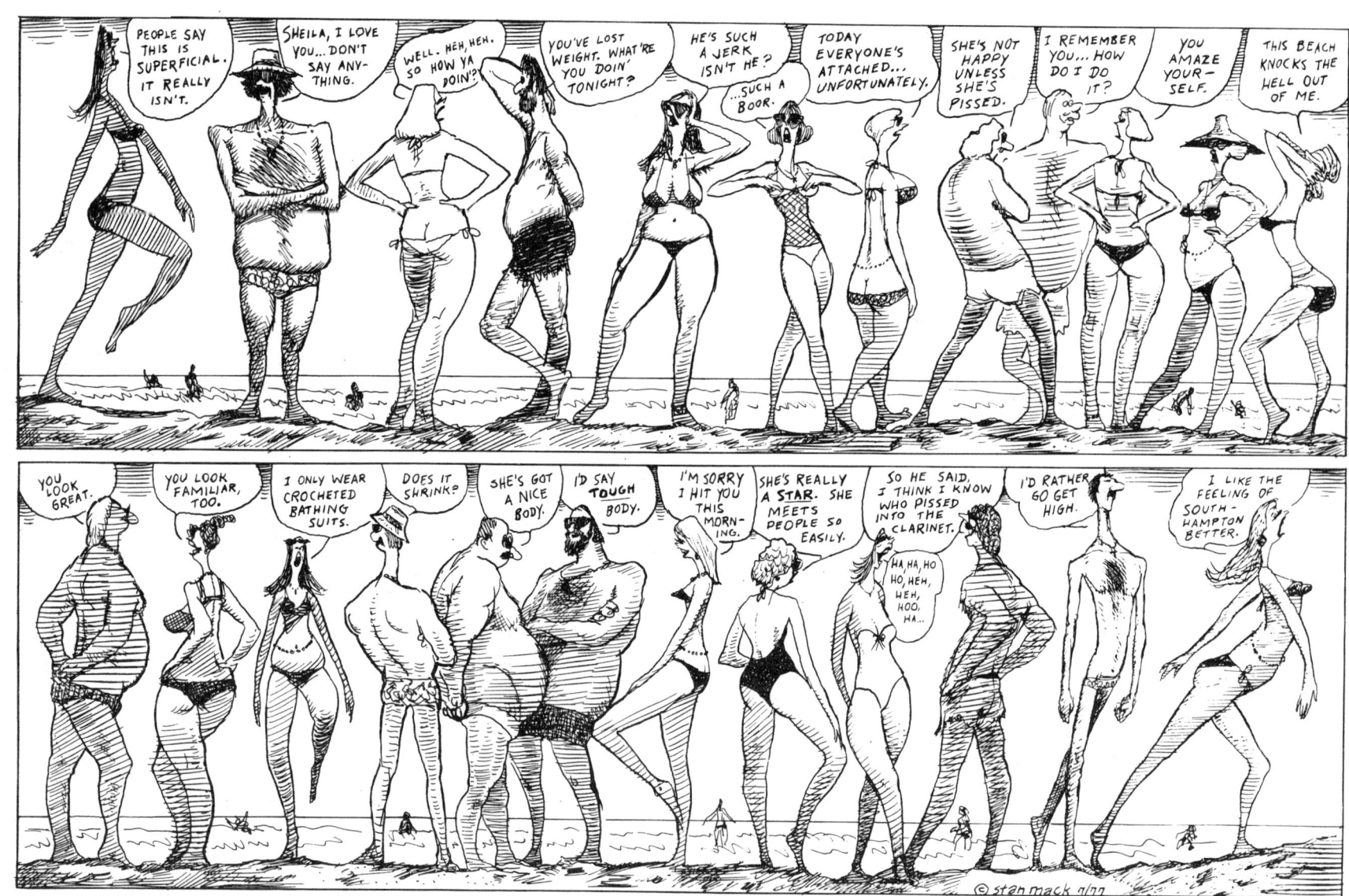

The Pink Pussy Cat Revisited

The Day the City Council Tried to Give Itself a Raise

A Holiday Tale